Thomas Cadell, John Brown, James Burnett Monboddo

Letters on the Italian Opera

Thomas Cadell, John Brown, James Burnett Monboddo

Letters on the Italian Opera

ISBN/EAN: 9783744691543

Printed in Europe, USA, Canada, Australia, Japan

Cover: Foto ©Thomas Meinert / pixelio.de

More available books at **www.hansebooks.com**

LETTERS

ON THE

ITALIAN OPERA:

ADDRESSED TO

The Hon. Lord MONBODDO.

BY THE LATE

Mr. JOHN BROWN.

SECOND EDITION.

LONDON:

Sold by T. CADELL, Strand.

MDCCXCI.

E R R A T A.

P. 9. l. 11. *for* Il volarmi *read* Involarmi.
P. 63. l. 14. *for* te *read* ti.
 Ibid. l. 15. *for* l'ammiro *read* t'ammiro.
 Ibid. l. 16. *for* te *read* ti.
P. 80. l. 11. *for* Their *read* Here.
P. 91. l. 5. *for* miè *read* mi è.
P. 92. l. 3. *for* carefully *read* carelefsly.
P. 99. l. 2. *for* cambio *read* cambiò.
 Ibid. l. 13 *for* there *read* thou.
P. 102. l. 10 *for* fmanie *read* fmania.
P. 106. l. 7. *for* afcoltar *read* afcoltai.]
.P. 126. l. 6. *for* affected *read* effected.
P. 133. l. 1. *for* le *read* la.
 Ibid. l. 3. *for* aquifta *read* acquifta.

ADVERTISEMENT.

THIS little piece is the compofition of one of the greateft artifts that ever was in Scotland; who, befides his fuperior excellence in his profeffion, which was *Drawing*, the principal part of Painting, was very learned in all the Italian Arts; and particularly in their Poetry and Mufic, the fubject of this little work, more learned, I believe, than any man in Great Britain.

As

As Beauty is pretty much the fame
in all the Fine Arts, there being a
cognation, as Cicero expreffes it,
by which they are connected and
related more or lefs to one another,
Mr Brown has fhown, in this work,
that he knew very well what Beauty was in Writing as well as in o-
ther Arts; for there is in his ftile
a copioufnefs and elegance, and
withal an accuracy of expreffion,
which are feldom to be met with
in the compofitions of this age;
and, both for matter and ftile, I
will venture to fet this little piece
againft any thing that has been
written on the fubject of the Fine
Arts

Arts in modern times; and, I am
perfuaded, it would have been ftill
more perfect in every refpect, if he
had lived to publifh it himfelf. He
has explained moft accurately every
thing belonging to the Italian Opera,
beginning with the *Recitative*, by
which the bufinefs or action of the
Opera, the principal thing in all
dramatic performances, is carried
on; and then proceeding to the
Airs or *Songs*, by which the fentiments and paffions of the *Dramatis
Perfonae* are expreffed. Thefe Airs
he has divided and explained fo
accurately as to fhow very clearly
' that there is no affection of the
' human

' human breaft,' (to ufe his own
words, and I cannot ufe better),
' from the flighteft and moft gen-
' tle ftirring of fentiment, to the
' moft frantic degree of paffion,
' which fome one of thefe claffes'
(of Airs) ' is not aptly fuited to
' exprefs *.' He has alfo fhown
how the defcriptive part in the
Opera is executed, and of what
good ufe the Orcheftra is there,
which is fo indifcreetly employed
in the Britifh Operas †. In this
paffage, he has very juftly cenfured
our tafte in Operas. And, in a-
nother

* Letter 8. in the beginning.
† Page 88. 89.

nother paſſage *, he has ſaid, that
' the admiration beſtowed in Bri-
' tain on difficulty and novelty, in
' preference to beauty and ſimpli-
' city, is the effect, not of the de-
' cline, but of the total want of
' taſte, and proceeds from the ſame
' principles with the admiration of
' tumbling and rope-dancing, which
' the multitude may gaze on with
' aſtoniſhment, long before they
' are ſuſceptible of the charms of
' graceful and elegant Pantomime,
' theſe feats of agility having ex-
' actly the ſame relation to fine
' dancing

* Page 115. 116.

' dancing that the above mentioned
' Airs have to expreſſive Muſic.'
And, in the ſame paſſage, he ob-
ſerves, that this admiration of the
new and difficult, which begins to
prevail in Italy, is a ſymptom of
the decline of the Arts there; ſo
that he appears to me to have had
a taſte, not only ſuperior to what
is to be found in Britain, but even
to the taſte at preſent in Italy, the
country of the Fine Arts; and I
have heard from others, as well as
from him, that the burletta, and
the taſte for the ridiculous, is pre-
vailing very much in Italy, than
which there can be no ſurer ſign of
the

the decline of genius and tafte in a nation. But the ferious Italian Opera, as he has defcribed it, and as it is acted in Rome, though it may not be fo perfect as it formerly was, is ftill the moft perfect junction of Poetry, Mufic, and Action, (or Dancing, as the ancients called it, which, among them, was an Art of Imitation, as well as Poetry and Mufic), the three fineft of the Fine Arts, that is now to be found in the world, and fuch as only can give us any idea of *Attic Tragedies, of ftatelieft and moft regal argument*, (to ufe an expreffion of Milton), with which that

learned

learned and elegant people were fo much delighted, and, upon the reprefentation of which they beftowed the greateft part of the revenue of their ftate. This work, therefore, of Mr Brown, will give great pleafure, not only to the Connoiſſeurs in Mufic, but alfo, I hope, to all the admirers of ancient Arts; and I am fure that all thofe who were acquainted with him, and knew him to be a man of great worth as well as genius, will be very glad to encourage this publication for the benefit of his widow and child.

L E T-

M R. BROWN was a native of Edinburgh, and was early de-ftined to take up the profeffion of a painter. He travelled into Italy, and at Rome met with Sir William Young and Mr. Townley, who, pleafed with fome very beautiful drawings done by him in pen and ink, took him with them, as a draftfman, into Sicily. Of the antiquities of this celebrated ifland he took feveral very fine views in pen and ink, exquifitely finifhed, yet ftill

b preferv-

preferving the character and fpirit of
the buildings he intended to reprefent.
He returned fome years afterwards from
Italy to his native town, where he was
much beloved and efteemed by many men
of letters, and by many women of elegance; his converfation being extremely acute and entertaining on moft fubjects, but peculiarly fo on thofe of art;
and his knowledge of mufic being very
great, and his tafte in it extremely juft
and refined. Lord Monboddo, with
that liberality which has ever charac-
terized him, gave him a general invita-
tion to his elegant and convivial table,
and employed him in making feveral
drawings in pencil for him. Mr. Brown,
however, in the year 1786, came to
London (that great emporium of talents

lents and abilities), and was greatly ca-
reffed by fcholars and men of tafte in
that metropolis, where he was very
much employed as a painter of fmall
portraits in black lead pencil, which
were always correctly drawn, and exhi-
bited, with a picturefque fidelity, the
features and character of the perfon who
fat to him. It is much to be lamented
that the public could make little ufe of
his talents, death depriving the public of
this very ingenious artift in 1787, after
a difeafe of great languor, which he bore
with that firmnefs of mind for which he
had been ever diftinguifhed through life.

Mr. Brown was not only known as an
exquifite draftfman, he was alfo a good
philofopher, a found fcholar, and endowed

dowed with a just and refined taste in all the liberal and polite Arts, and a man of consummate worth and integrity. Soon after his death these Letters on the Poety and Music of the Italian Opera, were first published for the benefit of his widow. They were originally written to his friend Lord Monboddo, who wished to have Mr. Brown's opinion on those subjects, which have so intimate a connection with his work on the Origin and Progress of Language; and who was so pleased with the style and observations contained in them, that he wrote an Introduction to them. The Letters are written with great elegance and perspicuity; they are most certainly the production of a strong and fervid mind, acquainted with the subject; and must

be

be of infinite utility to moſt of the fre-
quenters of the Italian Opera, by ena-
bling them to underſtand the reaſons on
which the pleaſure they receive at that
muſical performance is founded. They
were moſt aſſuredly not written for publication : they have, therefore, that
ſpirit and ſimplicity which every man
of genius diffuſes through any ſubject
of which he treats, and which he is but
too apt to refine away, when he ſeri-
ouſly ſits down to compoſe a work for the
Public. Lord Monboddo, in the fourth
Volume of the Origin and Progreſs of
language, ſpeaking of Mr. Brown, ſays,
" The account that I have given of the
Italian language is taken from one who
reſided above ten years in Italy ; and
who, beſides underſtanding the language

guage perfectly, is more learned in the Italian Arts of Painting, Sculpture, Mufic, and Poetry, than any man I ever met with. His natural good tafte he has improved by the ftudy of the monuments of ancient Art, to be feen at Rome and Florence; and as beauty in all the Arts is pretty much the fame, confifting of grandeur and fimplicity, variety, decorum, and a fuitablenefs to the fubject, I think he is a good judge of Language, and of Writing, as well as of Painting, Sculpture, and Mufic." Mr. Brown left behind him feveral very high finifhed Portraits in pencil, and many very exquifite Sketches in pencil and in pen and ink, which he had taken of perfons and of places in Italy; particularly a book of Studies of Heads,

taken

taken from the life, an ineſtimable trea-
ſure to any Hiſtory Painter, as it would
have ſerved him as a common-place-
book for his pictures, the heads it contained being all of them Italian ones,
of great expreſſion, or of high character. He was ſo enraptured with his Art,
and ſo aſſiduous in the purſuit of it, that
he ſuffered no countenance of beauty,
grace, dignity, or expreſſion to paſs him
unnoticed; and to be enabled to poſſeſs merely a ſketch for himſelf, of any
ſubject that ſtruck his fancy, he would
make a preſent of a high-finiſhed drawing to the perſon who permitted his
head to be taken by him. The characteriſtics of his hand were delicacy,
correctneſs, and taſte, (as the drawings
he made from many of Mr. Townley's
beſt

beſt ſtatues very plainly evince.) Of his mind, the leading features were acuteneſs, liberality, and ſenſibility, joined to a character firm, vigorous, and energetic. The laſt efforts of this ingenious Artiſt were employed in making two very exquiſite drawings, the one from Mr. Townley's celebrated buſt of Homer, the other from a fine original buſt of Mr. Pope, in general ſuppoſed to have been the work of Ryſbrac. From theſe drawings two very beautiful engravings have been made by Mr. Bartolozzi and his pupil Mr. Bovi.

L E T-

LETTER I.

My Lord,

IN order to give your Lordſhip a
diſtinct idea, not only of the various kinds of verſe made uſe of by
the Italians in their Opera, but of the
principles alſo by which the application
of that variety is directed, I find it ne-
ceſſary to take into conſideration the
union of poetry and muſic, which is

A   pecu-

peculiar to this ſpecies of drama. The nature of this union ſeems to have been well underſtood by their beſt dramatic writers, and they have ſeldom loſt ſight of it in their works; whilſt thoſe of our poets, who have written Cantatas or other compoſitions for muſic, appear either to have been not at all acquainted with it, or, if they were, to have totally diſregarded it. The Italians have, with great propriety, conſidered, that the ſpeeches in the drama, whether in dialogue or ſolilo-quy, muſt be either ſuch as are ex-preſſive of paſſion and ſentiment, or ſuch as are not ſo. On this real di-ſtinction, and not, as with us, on the mere caprice of the compoſer, is found-

ed

ed their firſt great diviſion of vocal
muſic into *recitative* and *air*. It is e-
vident, on the ſlighteſt conſideration,
that, in the progreſs of the drama,
many paſſages muſt neceſſarily occur,
ſuch as ſimple narration of facts, di-
rections given, plain anſwers made to
plain queſtions, ſometimes abſtract
truths or moral reflections;—none of
which, as they contain nothing of
paſſion or ſentiment, can ever become
the ſubject of muſical expreſſion. Sim-
ply to have ſpoken theſe paſſages, however, and then abruptly to have ſet
up a ſinging, when any pathetic part
preſented itſelf, would have produced
exactly that barbarous jumble of proſe
and poetry, of muſic and diſſonance,
which

which characterizes the Englifh comic
opera. To avoid this, and, at the fame
time, not idly to beftow the charms
of fancy and feeling, where embellifh-
ment and expreffion would be improper, the Italians have invented that
fpecies of finging termed by them *fimple recitative.* Its name almoft fuffici-
ently explains its nature: It is a fucceffion of notes fo arranged as to coin-
cide with the laws of harmony, tho'
never accompanied but by a fingle
inftrument, whofe office is merely to
fupport the voice, and to direct it in
its modulations. Though, for the fake
of this accompanyment, recitative is,
like other mufic, divided into bars,
yet are not thefe bars, as in other
mufic,

mufic, neceffarily of equal lengths; the notes of which they are compofed being fubjeɛted to no precife mufical meafure, but regulated, in this re-fpeɛt, almoft wholly by the natural profody of the language. Thus, this kind of recitative anfwers completely its end: It detains the audience very little longer than the fpoken recital would do; and, being mufic itfelf, the tranfition from it to the higher and more interefting parts is perfeɛtly na-tural, and agreeable to the ear.*

The

* According to your Lordfhip's opinion that there is fcarcely any fuch thing as long and fhort fyllables in modern languages, the notes of the Italian recitative would be all

of

The verſe appropriated to recitative
is of a mixed kind, conſiſting of the
heroic

of equal lengths. To obviate this objeċtion,
I muſt take notice, that what your Lordſhip
would call the *accented* ſyllable, they eſteem
the *long* one ; and whatever may be the caſe
in ſpeech, in pronouncing the recitative, they
moſt certainly render it longer, in the proportion, generally, of *two* to *one*. Thus, the
words *ămō, tălōr, cĕdē, fĭnī, tŏrnāi*, in which
the accent is laid on the laſt ſyllable, are, in
recitative, poſitively iambics, the firſt ſyllable being expreſſed by a quaver, the other by
a crotchet, thus, *ămō, tălōr*, &c. the laſt of
$$ \textquaver\ \textcrotchet \quad \textquaver\ \textcrotchet $$
which charaċters is the ſign of a duration of
time, exaċtly double the length of that denoted
by the firſt. Thoſe again which have the accent

heroic line of eleven fyllables, and of
a line of feven fyllables, with now and
then

cent on the firft fyllable, as *āmŏ, bēnĕ, cǐēlŏ,*
trōmbă, are trochaics. All the Articles of
two fyllables, fuch as *delle, alli,* &c. and the
Pronouns perfonal when joined with another
monofyllable, fuch as *mene, celo, vela, tiſſi,*
glielo, &c. may, with the ftricteft propriety,
be confidered as each a pyrrhic foot, which,
in recitative, would accordingly be expreſſéd
by two quavers, *mĕnĕ, cĕlŏ,* &c. The words
dŏcĭlĕ, flēbĭlĕ, mōrmŏră, are thus real dactyles,
whilft fuch as thefe again, *tĭmōrĕ, ŏnōrĕ,* &c.
are,

then a rhyme. In the intermingling,
however, thefe lines with each other,
as

are, to all intents and purpofes, each a foot,
confifting of a fhort, a long, and a fhort fyllable. Nay, I may go fo far as to fay, that no
fpecies of foot occurs in the ancient poetry
which is not frequently to be found in the
Italian recitative, in which three fucceffive
fhort, three fucceffive long fyllables, and often
four of each are to be found, and, indeed,
all the poffible varieties in which long and
fhort fyllables can be combined together.
Now, though it be allowed that the Italian
verfe is formed, not by the number of feet,
but of fyllables, it is fair to conclude, that this
manner of reciting it, by which not only various combinations of them are formed, but
their refpective length and brevity pofitively
afcer-

as well as with refpeƈt to the introduƈtion of the rhymes, the poet is
entirely left to the guidance of his
own ear and fentiment. This kind of
mixed verfe, from the variety of the
cadences which it affords, feems well
calculated to give to the recitative as
marked a refemblance to common
fpeech as is confiftent with the dignity
and beauty of numbers; whilft the fparing and judicious introduƈtion of
rhyme, either to finifh more highly
fome beautiful paffage, or more ftrongly
to point fome remarkable affertion or

B refleƈtion,

afcertained, muft not only give additional beauty
and variety to the verfe, but render the pronunciation itfelf more clear and explicit.

reflection, ferves to preferve throughout the piece a proper degree of u-
nity of effect, by preventing that irk-
fome and unnatural diffimilarity between the recitative and the airs, which
would, in fome degree, be the confequence of the want of this kind of
medium.   Upon the whole, it appears
admirably well fuited to the lefs important parts of a production fo refined
and artificial as the Opera, whofe object, like that of the arts of painting
and fculpture amongft the ancients, is
not fo much the exact imitation of
nature, as the union in as high a degree as poffible of what is beautiful
with what is natural.

LETTER

LETTER II.

My Lord,

IN the former fheets I have endeavoured to explain to your Lordfhip the nature of fimple recitative, and
to defcribe the kind of verfe appropriated to it. I proceed now to treat
of the higher parts of vocal mufic,
thofe, namely, which are adapted to
the more interefting and pathetic paffages of the drama. With refpect to
thefe,

thefe, diftinctions have been likewife
made by the Italians, which feem
perfectly well founded. They muft,
in the firft place, have obferved, that
all thofe paffages in which the mind
of the fpeaker is agitated by a rapid
fucceffion of various emotions, are,
from their nature, incompatible with
any particular ftrain, or length of melody; for that which conftitutes fuch
particular ftrain is the relation of feveral parts to one whole. Now, it is
this whole which the Italians diftinguifh
by the name of *motivo*, which may be
tranflated *ftrain,* or *fubject of the air,*
and which they conceive to be incon-
fiftent with the brevity and defultory
fenfe of thofe ejaculations, which are
the

the effect of a high degree of agitation.
Air they think even inadmiffible in thofe
paffages, in which, though the emotions
be not various, yet the fentences are
broken and incoherent. To give an
inftance: The following fpeech, tho'
terror be uniformly expreffed by the
whole of it, feems not at all a fubject
fit to be comprehended under, or expreffed by one regular ftrain :

Bring me unto my trial when you will.—
Dy'd he not in his bed?—Where fhould he die?
Oh! torture me no more—I will confefs.—
Alive again!—then fhew me wh're he is ;
I'll give a thoufand pounds to look on him.
—He hath no eyes ;—the duft hath blinded
  them—

       Comb

Comb down his hair—look! look! it ftands up-
   right
Like lime-twigs fet to catch my winged foul.——
Give me fome drink, &c.——

SHAKESPEARE's Henry VI.

But, whilft the Italians conceived
fuch paffages to be incompatible with
that regularity of meafure, and that u-
nity of ftrain which is effential to air,
they felt, however, that they were of
all others the moft proper fubject for
mufical expreffion : And, accordingly,
both the poet and mufician feem, by
mutual confent, to have beftowed on
fuch paffages their chief ftudy ; and the
mufician, in particular, never fails to
exert on them his higheft and moft
brilliant

brilliant powers. It is to them they adapt that fpecics of recitative termed *recitativo iftrumentato*, or *recitativo obligato,* — *accompanied recitative.* In this kind of recitative the finger is, in a more fpecial manner, left to the dictates of his own feelings and judgment with refpect to the meafure: He muft not indeed reverfe the natural profody of the language, by making fhort what fhould be long, or *vice verfa*; but he may not only proportionally lengthen the duration of each fyllable, but he may give to particular fyllables what length he pleafes, and precipitate confiderably the pronunciation of others, juft as he thinks the expreffion requires. The march of the

notes

notes is very different in this from that of the common or fimple recitative; delicacy, pathos, force, dignity, according to the different expreffions of the words, are its chara&teriftics. It is in this fpecies of fong that the fineft effe&ts of the chromatic, and, as far as our fyftem of mufical intervals is fufceptible of it, even of the enharmonic fcale, are peculiarly felt; and it is here alfo that the powers of modulation are moft happily, becaufe moft properly, employed, by changes of tone analogous to the variety of the matter, in a wonderful manner enforcing and chara&terizing the tranfitions which are made from one fubje&t or emotion to another. Here, too, the whole orcheftra

lends

lends its aid; nor are the inftruments limited to the fimple duty of fupport-ing and directing the voice. In this high fpecies of recitative it is the peculiar province of the inftrumental parts, during thofe paufes which naturally take place between the burfts of paffion which a mind ftrongly agitated breaks into, to produce fuch founds as ferve to awake in the audience fenfations and emotions fimilar to thofe which are fuppofed to agitate the fpeaker. Here, again, another fine diftinction is made by the Italians, between the defcriptive and the pathetic powers of mufic. Thefe laft are proper to the voice, the former to the orcheftra alone. Thus, the fymphonies which accompany this

C   kind

kind of recitative, befides the general analogy they muft have to the imme- diate fentiments, and even to the cha- racter, of the fpeaker, are often parti- cularly defcriptive of the place in which he is, or of fome other concomitant circumftance which may ferve to heigh- ten the effect of the fpeech itfelf. Sup- pofe, for example, the fcene to be a prifon ; the fymphonies, whilft they accord with the general tenor of the words, will paint, if I may be allowed the expreffion, the horrors of the dun- geon itfelf :—And I can affure your Lordfhip that I have heard fymphonies of this kind ftrongly expreffive of fuch horrors. Again, fuppofe the fcene by moon-light and the general tone of the

the paffion plaintive, the fweetnefs, the
ferenity, and, (though to thofe, who
have never experienced the effects of
mufic in this degree, it may feem pa-
radoxical to fay fo), even the folitude,
nay, the filence of the fcene, would
make part of the ideas fuggefted by
the fymphonies. Should a ftorm be
introduced, the fkilful compofer would
contrive to make the rain beat, and
the tempeft howl moft fearfully, by
means of the orcheftra : Nay, in a
fcene fuch as that of the dying Beau-
fort, which I have quoted above * to
your Lordfhip, the mufician, following clofe the wild ravings of the fpeaker, would, during the paufes of the
                                     fpeech,

* Page 13.

ſpeech, call forth from the inſtruments
ſuch ſounds as would thrill with terror
the audience, by realizing, in a manner, to their ſenſe and feeling, the hor-
rible apprehenſions of his diſtracted
mind. But the combined powers of
melody and harmony are never more
effectually felt than when, in this kind
of recitative, they are employed to
mark ſome very ſtriking tranſition. In
a ſcene of madneſs, for example, where
the imagination of the ſpeaker is ſuppoſed to ſtart from a gloomy deſart to
flowery meads, the orcheſtra would,
by an immediate change of meaſure,
of melody, of harmony, perhaps of
ſounds too, mark the tranſition—would
proceed to ſpread out the ſmiling land-
ſkip, to adorn it with gayeſt flowers,

.to

to awake the zephyr, and, in fhort, give to the audience, by means of a wonderful analogy of founds, the moft lively reprefentation of the new image which is fuppofed to have taken poffeffion of the madman's mind.—Thefe are effects of what I have ventured to call the Defcriptive, or Imitative, powers of mufic. With refpect to the tranfitions of paffion, fuch as from tendernefs to jealoufy, from joy to anger, &c. thefe belong to the Pathetic powers of mufic, and are the peculiar province of the vocal part. Often, in the middle of a very agitated Recitative, on the occurrence of fome tender idea, on which the mind is fuppofed to dwell with a kind of melancholy pleafure,

the

the mufic lofes, by degrees, the irregular character of Recitative, and re-
folves gradually into the even meafure
and continued melody of Air,—then,
on a fudden, at the call of fome idea
of an oppofite nature, breaks off again
into its former irregularity. This change
from Recitative to Air, and thence to
Recitative again, never fails, when properly introduced, to have a very ftriking and beautiful effect. Whilft it is
the bufinefs of the orcheftra thus clofely
to accompany the fentiments and fitua-
tion of the finger, the actor, in his
turn, as there is no note without a
meaning, muft be continually attentive
to the orcheftra: During thofe intervals, in which the inftruments may be

faid.

faid to fpeak, his action muft be in
ftrick concert with the mufic; every
thing muft tend to the fame point; fo
that the poet, the mufician, the actor,
muft all feem to be informed by one
foul.——If your Lordfhip, to the natural voice of paffion, and the proper
and graceful expreffion of action, ima-
gines, thus united, the intrinfic charm
of found itfelf, and the wonderful powers of melody and harmony, I hope
you will join with me in opinion, that
the effect produced by fuch union is
much richer, much more beautiful,
much more powerful and affecting,
than any that can be produced by fimple declamation. Though, in paffages
of this defcription, the language ought
certainly

certainly to rife with the fubject, yet
the verfe which is here made ufe of, is
of the fame kind with that employed
in the common Recitative, as being that
which has the greateft variety, and fuf-
fers the feweft reftrictions, and, as fuch,
the beft adapted to the irregular nature
of fuch paffages.——Having thus endeavoured to explain to your Lordfhip
the nature of *recitative, fimple and accompanied*, of thofe diftinctions on
which they are refpectively founded,
and of the fpecies of verfe in which
they are written, I proceed to treat of
Air, and of the different kinds of verfi-
fication which are employed in it. As
to the principles which direct the choice
in adapting particular meafures to particular

ticular airs, I fhall have nothing to fay, they being exactly the fame with thofe by which the lyric poet adapts the verfe to the various fubject of an ode ;—the heroic to the grave and fublime ;— that which ftill partakes of dignity, though rather fmooth than grand, to the tender and pathetic ;—that which is more violent and unequal, to the highly impaffioned parts ;—and that which is of the airy dancing kind, to the lighter and more lively paffages of the piece: Diftinctions, which, it may be obferved, are evidently confequences of the original union of poetry and mufic.

I am well aware, that great part of what I have here faid of the power of

D   the

the Italian mufic would, to many, perhaps to moft people, appear the language rather of enthufiafm than of any
thing elfe : Perhaps it partly is fo ; for
my own feelings, on the authority alone
of which I fpeak, may, in fome degree,
proceed from enthufiafm. Whether
this be the cafe, or whether the effects
I mention be completely real, but take
place in confequence of certain fenfibi-
lities, fo partially diftributed among
mankind, that, perhaps, even the leffer
number are fufceptible of thefe effects,
I do not prefume to determine. If
this laft be the cafe, (and there is no
abfurdity in fuppofing it to be fo), it is
evident, however, that thofe who pro-
fefs fo great a degree of fenfibility to
the

the powers of mufic, will be very apt
to appear affected and enthufiaftic to
the reft of mankind, who are, furely,
in fome degree, juftified for calling in
queftion the exiftence of pleafures to
which, poffeffing the fame organs, all
in feeming equal perfection, they find
themfelves perfect ftrangers: Whilft,
on the other hand, thofe who acknow-
ledge the power of mufic, will think
they have a complete right to affert the
reality of that of which they have fo
feeling a conviction. For my own
part, I am firmly perfuaded, that what
I have ventured to advance to your
Lordfhip touching the effects of mufic,
is not at all exaggerated with refpect to
the feelings of thoufands befides myfelf

felf: Nay, it is my opinion, that, were
muſical entertainments arrivẹd to that
degree of perfection to which they
might be brought, they could not fail
of producing effects much more powerful than any I ever had an opportunity of experiencing.

LETTER

LETTER III.

My Lord,

REcitative and Air may be considered as *genera* in music, and
the different kinds of each as *species.*

What I have already had the honour
of submitting to your Lordship's peru-
sal, on the subject of Recitative, may
serve partly to explain the nature of
Air.   All those passages where the
transi-

tranſition from one emotion to another
is ſudden and violent, and which,
therefore, can neither, on account of
their brevity, make each a whole of itſelf, nor, by reaſon of their variety, be
made parts of the ſame whole, are ex-
preſſed in Recitative. Thoſe, on the
other hand, in which one ſentiment
pervades a whole ſentence compoſed
of different parts, become proper ſub-
jects for Air ; and, indeed, every complete muſical ſtrain may, with great
juſtneſs, be termed a ſentence or pe-
riod in melody.——Before proceeding
to ſpeak of the different kinds of Airs,
it may not be improper to ſay ſome-
thing of the Symphony by which they
are in general preceded. This Symphony

phony is the enunciation, by the orcheſtra, of the ſtrain or ſubject, what
the Italians call the *motivo* of the Air;
and when not improperly introduced,
(which it always is when the ſenſe admits not of any pauſe), ſerves ſeveral
uſeful purpoſes;—it gives time to the
ſinger to breathe, already, perhaps, fa-
tigued by a long recitative;—it often
fills up, with propriety, a natural pauſe,
and always finely prepares the audience for what is to come after, by e-
nabling them, having thus once heard
the ſtrain, to liſten with more intelli-
gence, and, of conſequence, with more
intereſt and pleaſure to the ſong. Beſides, the general *uſe* of the Symphony,
renders the *omiſſion* of it, on particular

occa-

occafions, beautiful and ftriking.——
Thus, for example, at the end of a
Recitative, or at the beginning of a
fcene, when the audience are expecting,
as ufual, the preparatory Symphony to
the Air, they are fuddenly furprifed by
the violent burft of fome impetuous
paffion, which admitted of no poffible
paufe. The propriety of having, in
fuch a circumftance, omitted the Symphony, comes forcibly on the mind,
as, *vice verfa*, the effect of the omif-
fion here confirms the propriety of u-
fing it where the fenfe allows it to be
introduced. Sometimes, again, the
Symphony is omitted in a very different manner, tho' with equal propriety:
When, for inftance, in an accompanied

nied recitative, after a fucceffion of very different emotions, fome fentiment is fuppofed to take poffeffion of the mind, related to that which is to be the fubject of the Air, and to which it is afterwards led by a gradation of kindred emotions.:—The progrefs, in this cafe, from Recitative to Air, is fo gentle, that the audience frequently find themfelves melting into tears at the affecting and continued melody of the Air, before they are aware that the Recitative is ended. This imperceptible tranfition is effected fometime by fubjecting the recitative itfelf to mufical meafure, and making the notes of it, by degrees, take a refemblance to thofe of the Air. At other times,

E   it

it is brought about by introducing,
in the inftrumental parts, during the
paufes of the Recitative, paffages of the
ftrain which is to make the fubject of
.the Air: Sometimes by both thefe
means. The effect of this gradual
tranfition is always very fine, and, as
your Lordfhip will obferve, is, in part,
derived from that habitual diftinction
which the audience are accuftomed to
make between Recitative and Air.—As
to the Airs themfelves, your Lordfhip
will conceive that they are as various
as their fubjects. Thefe are every poffible fentiment, affection, or paffion,
the expreffion of which is extended
through one fentence of a certain
length; fuch fentences as thefe,—*I
love*

*love—I fear his wrath—I mourn her·
lofs*—though all proper fubjects for
mufical expreffion, being evidently too
fhort to afford matter for a ftrain or
melody, which, however fimple, muft
ftill be compofed of parts, the relations
of which to one another, and to one
whole, conftitute, indeed, the effence
of fuch ftrain.—The Air, though it
muft contain at leaft one complete fentence, is not, however, limited to one
alone: It is often compofed of two,
fometimes of more parts; but thefe,
whether related by analogy or by con-
traft to the principal one, muft each
ftrictly belong to the fame whole.
The Airs are divided, by the Italians,
into certain claffes; thefe claffes are
origi-

originally founded on real diftinctions, drawn from the nature of the various affections of the mind ; but muficians, who, like other artifts, are feldom philofophers, have diftinguifhed them by names relative to the practice of their own profeffion.—The principal are the following :

Aria Cantabile,—by pre-eminence fo called, as if it alone were Song : And, indeed, it is the only kind of fong which gives the finger an opportunity of difplaying at once, and in the higheft degree, all his powers, of whatever defcription they be. The proper fubjects for this Air are fentiments of tendernefs.

Aria

Aria di portamento,—a denomination expreffive of the carriage, (as they thus call it), of the voice. This kind of Air is chiefly compofed of long notes, fuch as the finger can dwell on, and have, thereby, an opportunity of more effectually difplaying the beauties, and calling forth the powers of his voice; for the beauty of found itfelf, and of voice in particular, as being the fineft of all founds, is held, by the Italians, to be one of the chief fources of the pleafure we derive from mufic. The fubjects proper for this Air are fentiments of dignity.

Aria di mezzo carattere.—Your Lordfhip can be at no lofs to underftand

this

this term ; though I know no words in our language by which I could properly tranflate it. It is a fpecies of Air, which, though expreffive neither of the dignity of this laft, nor of the pathos of the former, is, however, ferious and pleafing.

Aria parlante,—fpeaking Air, is that which, from the nature of its fubject, admits neither of long notes in the compofition, nor of many ornaments in the execution. The rapidity of the motion of this Air is proportioned to the violence of the paffion which is expreffed by it. This fpecies of Air goes fometimes by the name of *aria di nota e parola,* and likewife of *aria agitata;*

but

but thefe are rather fub-divifions of the
fpecies, and relate to the different degrees of violence of the paffion expreffed.

Aria di bravura, aria di agilita,—is
that which is compofed *chiefly*, indeed,
too often, *merely* to indulge the finger
in the difplay of certain powers in the
execution, particularly extraordinary
agility or compafs of voice. Though
this kind of air may be fometimes introduced with fome effect, and without any great violation of propriety,
yet, in general, the means are here
confounded with the end.

Rondo

Rondo—is a term of French origin, unknown, I believe, till of late to the Italian muficians. It relates merely to a certain peculiarity in the conftruction of the fong, in which the compofer, after having properly eftablifhed the fubject, carries it through a variety of tones, every now and then returning to the principal ftrain or part, and always concluding with it.

Cavatina—is an expreffion which likewife relates to the form alone, meaning an Air of one part, without repetition.

Thefe, to the beft of my remembrance, are the claffes into which the Italians have divided Air.

I

I fhall now fay fomething of each
clafs; and, in doing fo, I hope to give
your Lordfhip fome idea of the great
extent as well as precifion of the Italian mufic, and to fhow, that, though
the names of thefe claffes be evidently
taken from circumftances of practice,
yet thefe circumftances, if properly attended to, will be found to be ftrictly
connected with, and, indeed, to ori-
ginate from diftinctions of a higher
kind, which muft have been previouf-
ly made with refpect to the nature of
the paffions, and their effect on utterance and expreffion. Whether the I-
talian compofers, in obferving thefe
diftinctions, have been guided by fome
fyftem, or have been merely influenced

F   by

by feeling, I cannot take upon me to fay. I am rather, however, inclined to think that the latter is the cafe; in the firft place, becaufe I never heard of any fuch fyftem exifting among them, and, becaufe I have been perfonally acquainted with feveral of their fineft compofers now living, that had no idea of it; and, again, becaufe I think, that, to the want of fuch a fyftem can be alone attributed the grofs deviations (which, even in the works of their greateft mafters, are fometimes to be met with), from its moft obvious and moft effential principles.

LETTER

LETTER IV.

My Lord,

THE *aria cantabile* is emphatically fo called, as being the higheft fpecies of Song. It is that indeed which affords the finger an opportunity of difplaying, in the execution of it, all his powers and fkill ;—if he has voice, if he has feeling, if he has tafte, if he has fancy, if he has fcience— here he has ample fcope for the exertion
tion

tion of them all. The subject proper for this air is the expreſſion of tender-neſs. Though this be an expreſſion which always tends to ſadneſs, yet the ſadneſs is of that pleaſing kind which the mind loves to indulge: Thus, the memory of pleaſures that are paſt, the complaints of a lover abſent from his *faithful* miſtreſs, and ſuch like, are proper themes for this air. Hence it ariſes, that the *aria cantabile*, whilſt it is ſuſceptible of great pathos, admits, without prejudice to the expreſſion, of being highly ornamented; for this plain reaſon, that, though the ſenti-ments it expreſſes are affecting, they are, at the ſame time, ſuch as the mind dwells on with pleaſure; and it is like-wiſe

wife for this reafon that the fubject of
the *cantabile* muft never border on deep
diftrefs, nor approach to violent agitation, both of which are evidently in-
confiftent with ornament. The motion
of this air, though not fo folemn as that
which belongs to ftill graver fubjects,
is very flow, and its conftituent notes,
of confequence, proportionally long;
I fay *conftituent notes*, in order to diftinguifh thofe which the finger introduces
as ornamental from thofe which conftitute the melody itfelf. Thefe laft
are, in general, very few, extremely
fimple in their march, and fo arranged
as to allow great latitude to the fkill of
the finger. The inftrumental parts
are, in this kind of fong, reftricted to
almoft

almoſt nothing; for, though the accompanyment is of uſe to the ſinger becauſe it ſupports the voice, yet ought it to be kept ſo ſubordinate to the vocal part, as never, during the ſong, to become the objeƈt of attention. The ſinger who attempts the *cantabile* ſhould be endowed, in the firſt place, with a fine voice, of the ſweet and plaintive kind, that the long notes, of which this ſong is compoſed, may, of themſelves, delight the ear: He ought to have great ſenſibility, that he may nicely feel and expreſs in an affeƈting manner the ſentiment: He ſhould poſſeſs, beſides, great taſte and fancy, highly to ornament the melody, and, thereby, give to it that elegance which

is

is effential to this kind of fong: An accurate judgment is likewife neceffary, to keep his fancy within due bounds; and he ought to be a perfect mafter of the fcience of counter-point, that he may know precifely what liberties he may take with refpect to the harmony of the other parts. As the productions of *fcience* are, at leaft in part, juftly efteemed by the degree of *utility* which attends them, fo thofe of *art* may be by the degree of *pleafure* they afford. Now, it is the fuperior degree of plea-fure (which proceeds from the joint exertion of fo many powers of nature and art in the *aria cantabile*) that gives to it the pre-eminence over every other kind of fong; for your Lordfhip will

obferve,

obferve, that, in liftening to an air
of this defcription, though the mind
is all awake to feeling, yet are the e-
motions it experiences of that gentle
kind which unfit it neither for the con-
templation of beauty, nor for the admiration of art; on the contrary, they
ferve to difpofe it more effectually for
both. Thus, many of the nobleft fa-
culties of the mind are gratified at
once; we judge, we admire, we feel,
at the fame inftant of time; and, I
may even fay, we are, at the fame inftant, fenfibly feafted; for there is no
doubt but there is a charm, not only
in the harmony of founds, but even in
the beauty of found itfelf, which acts
phyfically on the machine, and may

be

be confidered as actually producing a
fenfual gratification. The following
are examples of the *cantabile* from Metaftafio: In the firft, a lover, complain-
ing to his friend of the cruelty of his
miftrefs, concludes the recitative by
faying,

Ma quanto, ah, tu nol fai, quant' è tiranna.

But thou knoweft not, alas! how unkind
fhe is.

A I R.

Jo lo fo, che il bel fembiante
Un iftante, oh dio, mirai,
E mai piu da quell 'iftante
Non lafciai di fofpirar.

G

I know it, who, but for a moment, be-
held that lovely countenance; and never,
from that moment, have ceafed to figh.

Jo lo fo ; lo fanno quefte
Valli ombrofe, erme forefte,
Che han d'a me quel nome amato,
Imparato a replicar.

I know it; and thefe fhady vales, thefe fo-
litary woods, which have learned from me
to repeat her beloved name, know it alfo.

In this fecond, a young warrior, a-
bout to take leave of his weeping miftrefs, thus addreffes her :

Frena le belle lagrime,
Idolo del mio cor;

No,

No, per vederti piangere,
Cara, non ò valor;
Ah non deftarmi almeno
Nuovi tumulti in feno;
Baftano i dolci palpiti
Che vi cagiona amor.

Ceafe thofe gentle tears, my foul's idol; if I fee thee weep, my fortitude forfakes me. Ah, forbear to awake in my bofom new tumults; the foft palpitations are fufficient which love caufes there already.

I have only now to add, on the fubject of this air, that I fhould be forry, from what I have faid of the ornament effential to it, to have given rife to an opinion in your Lordfhip, which the general practice of fingers is, I own,
                                        but

but too apt to confirm, namely, that the *cantabile* is little elfe than a ftring of flourifhes, originating almoft entirely in the caprice of the performer. This is very far from being the cafe: Though the melancholy exprefled by the *cantabile* be of that foothing kind which the mind loves to indulge, and is, therefore, not incompatible with fome exertions of the fancy, yet are thefe exertions clearly limited, both with refpect to number and quality, by the fenfe of the words; fome admit of more, fome of lefs ornament. The expreffion of tendernefs, as has been already obferved, is that which peculiarly characterifes this air; and juft in proportion as this expreffion is

allied

allied to fentiments of hope or pleafure, or tends rather towards fadnefs
and defpondency, it admits more or
lefs of being ornamented.—As to the
exact quantum, no precife rules can be
given:—This, it is evident, muft always
depend on the nice judgment of the
performer; and it is certain, that, the
greater his feeling, and the more cor-
rect his tafte, the more fparing he will
be in the application of embellifhments.
—Thofe, he makes ufe of, will refemble
in kind and number; not thofe ornaments which, without diftinction, o-
verload the whole furface of a Gothic
building, but thofe with which the
Greeks adorned their architecture,
which, in times of the pureft tafte,

were

were never fo many as to difguife, in any degree, the appearance of fimplicity, nor fo prominent as to difturb the fymmetry of the great component parts of the edifice. Having mentioned architecture, a very ftriking analogy prefents itfelf to me between the Corinthian order and the *aria cantabile.*

As in this order it appears evidently to have been the intention of the inventor to unite, as far as they are confiftent with each other, beauty and utility; fo it feems the object of the *cantabile* to unite, in the fame manner, beauty and expreffion. Thus, elegance and refinement are equally the character of both,—in both have the

fame

fame kind of limitation;—in the former, any thing, however beautiful in
itfelf, that militated againft utility,
would have been inadmiffible;—in the
latter, any ornament, however graceful
in itfelf, that ran counter-to, or, in the
leaft, diminifhed the expreffion, would
be unpardonable;—for utility is the
firft principle of architecture, and expreffion is the great end of mufic.
This analogy might be carried a great
deal farther, but, I am afraid, I have
already exhaufted your Lordfhip's pa-
tience.

LETTER

LETTER V.

My Lord,

THE second class of Airs to be considered, is the *aria di portamento,*
—a term expressive of a certain way of managing the voice. It means, that the voice must be strongly supported, and artfully managed, through the long notes, of which this air is composed, the motion of which is graver than that of any other species. In the

H   *cantabile*

cantabile the notes are alſo long; but their march is, in general, gradual and gliding: Here, on the contrary, the intervals ought to be bold, ſtriking, and unexpected. In the former, the gentle dying away,—here, the grand ſwell of the voice ought to be princi-pally attended to. In ſhort, pathos and elegance are the characteriſtics of the *cantabile*,—grandeur and ſublimity of the *portamento.* The great object, which muſicians ſeem to have had in view in this kind of air, is to give full ſcope to the voice to diſplay, in the higheſt degree, its powers and beau-ties;—as the Italians very emphatically expreſs it, " far pompa della voce." In the general definition of this air, I

took

took notice to your Lordſhip of the high value which the Italians put on the beauty of voice itſelf; and, indeed, the effect of a powerful, and, at the ſame time, harmonious voice, in the execution of an air of this kind, is ſuch, as, I believe, muſt be felt before it can be conceived.

Every ſentiment, which proceeds from greatneſs of mind, or that ſpeaks the admiration of what is itſelf ſublime, is a proper ground-work for this air. The ſentiment expreſſed by it may be accompanied with ſenſibility, but muſt be calm, and undiſturbed by paſſion. This being the caſe, your Lordſhip will ſee, that the ſubject of the *porta-mento*

mento is of a nature too serious and important to admit of that degree of ornament which is essential to the *cantabile*. Like the Doric order in architecture, though it rejects not ornament altogether, yet it must owe its effect chiefly to its simplicity and grandeur. If your Lordship will allow me, in another way, to illustrate the specific difference of these two classes, I might say that, were Venus to sing, her mode of song would be the *cantabile*; the *portamento* would be that of the Queen of gods and men.

Your Lordship will be sensible, that, though the line between these two classes be distinctly drawn, yet they may,

may, more or lefs, partake, fometimes, of the nature of each other. Some fentiments, for example, of a female lover, all gentlenefs and fenfibility, may yet be accompanied with a degree of noblenefs, which, if properly felt by the compofer, may induce him to give a grandeur to the mufic that will make it partake, more than ufual, of the ftile of the *portamento*: As, on the other hand, circumftances may be i-magined in which the moft heroic fen-timents, from the mixture of fome tender affection, may, without lofing their dignity, be exprefled by ftrains fomewhat more approaching to the *cantabile* than the general character of the air allows: But thefe, indeed, are

nice

nice fhades of diftinction, which efcape
the controul of fixed rules, and can be
appretiated only by correfpondent feelings. The peculiar qualities neceffary
for the proper performance of this air
are, firft of all, a powerful and beautiful voice; for, without this, no fkill,
no tafte, no feeling even, can ever render long notes fupportable, much lefs
make them a fource of delight. Se-
condly, a clear and unequivocal pronunciation, by virtue of which, not-
withftanding the length of the notes,
the articulations, with which they be-
gan, may be fo ftrongly impreffed on the
memory, as to render the fenfe eafily
followed and underftood. Laftly, A
graceful manner of acting, without
which,

which, in that kind of " action fou-
" tenue," which the great length of
the notes requires, the deportment of
the actor muft indeed be aukward in
the extreme.

I proceed now to give your Lordfhip
fome examples of thefe airs, beginning
with one of the moft ferious kind,
and, by its nature, the fartheft removed
from the *cantabile* : — It is likewife
taken from Metaftafio :—In the Oratorio of *the paffion of Chrift* :

Dovunque il guardo giro,
Immenfo Dio, te vedo
Nell' opre tue l'ammiro,
Te reconofco in me.

Where'er

Where'er I turn my eyes, Great God, I fee thee ; I revere thee in thy works ; I feel thee in myfelf.

La terra, il mar, le sfere
Moftran il tuo potere ;
Tu fei per tutto, e noi
Tutti viviamo in te.

The earth, the fea, the heavens, fhew forth thy power ; thou art over all, and we all live in thee.

The following example is from the opera of Attilius Regulus, by the fame author. It is put in the mouth of the Roman Conful, on hearing Regulus infift on being fent back to Carthage.

Oh

Oh qual fiamma di glorià e d'onore
Sento fcorrer per tutte le vene,
Alma grande, parlando con te.

Oh! What a flame of glory and honour I
feel run through every vein, thou great foul,
in converfing with thee.

No, non vive fi timido core
Che in udirti, con quelle catene
Non cambiaffe la forte d'un re.

No, there lives not a foul fo vile, who, hearing thee, would not exchange with thefe chains
even the fortune of a monarch.

Here is a third from the fame opera:
—The daughter of Regulus feeing her
father fo much occupied by the great
I public

public object he had in view, that he appears dead to that paternal fondnefs which fhe had before experienced from him, fays,—

Ah! father, Why are you fo much changed?

To which he anfwers, clofing the re-citative,

My fortunes are changed,—I am ftill the fame.

A I R.

Non perdo la calma
Fra i ceppi, o gli allori :
Non va fino all' alma
La mia fervitu.

Whether

Whether bound in chains, or encircled with laurels, I lose not my serenity, my servitude reaches not the soul.

Combatte i rigori
Di forte incostante
In vario sembiante
L'istessa virtu.

The same virtue, under different appearances, combats the rigour of inconstant fortune.

LETTER

LETTER VI.

MY LORD,

THE *aria di mezzo carattere* comes next to be confidered. The fub-jects proper for this kind of air are many, and very different, its particular character being neither the pathetic, the grand, nor the paffionate, but the pleafing. There may be an almoft in-finite variety of fentiments, very pretty

and

and very interefting, which are not,
however, of fufficient importance to
be made the fubject either of the *can-*
tabile or the *portamento* :—The *aria di*
mezzo carattere comprehends all fuch.
—From the great variety which this
air, of confequence, embraces, as well
as from the lefs emphatic nature of the
fentiments to which it belongs, its general expreffion is not fo determined
as that of the former claffes; yet, with
refpect to each individual air, the expreffion is far from being vague or
dubious, and though fome greater latitude be here granted to the fancy of
the compofer, nothing is given to his
caprice, the fenfe itfelf of the words
clearly afcertaining, in point both of

degree

degree and quality, the expreſſion. The degree ought to be in exact proportion to the placidity or warmth of the ſentiment, and its particular caſt ought to be regulated by the nature of that paſſion to which the ſentiment is naturally allied ; for ſentiments are but gentler degrees of paſſion. Thus, this claſs of airs, whilſt it retains its own particular character, may, by turns, have ſome affinity with almoſt all the other claſſes ; but, whilſt its latitude is great in reſpect of variety, its limitations, with regard to degree, are obvious ;—it may be ſoothing, but not ſad ;—it may be pleaſing, but not elevated ;—it may be lively, but not gay. The motion of this air is, by the Italians,.

lians, termed *andante*, which is the exact medium of musical time between its extremes of slow and quick. As the vocal part is never suppofed here to be so beautiful and interesting as in the higher claffes, the orcheftra, tho' it ought never to cover the voice, is not, however, kept in such subordination to it;—it is not only allowed to play louder, but may be more frequently introduced by itself, and may, on the whole, contribute more to the general effect of the air.

This kind of song is admirably well calculated to give repose and relief to the mind, from the great degree of attention and (with respect to myself, at

leaft,

leaft, I might fay) agitation excited by
the higher and more pathetic parts of the
piece:—They poffefs the true character
which belongs to the fubordinate parts
of a beautiful whole, as affording a
repofe, not the effect of a total want
of intereft, but of an intereft which they
call forth of a different and more placid
kind, which the mind can attend to
with more eafe, and can enjoy without
being exhaufted. I could wifh it were
in my power to give here three or
four examples of this air, the more
clearly to evince to your Lordfhip that
this air, whilft it retains perfectly its
own peculiar character, may fometimes
approach, in its expreffion, the *cantabile*, fometimes the *portamento*, and

fome-

fometimes the *parlante*,—but having. but one volume of Metaftafio by me, I cannot make that feleƈtion of examples which I could wifh. 'The following is from the facred compofition of the death of Abel ; and, as your Lordfhip will obferve, partakes of the nature of the *cantabile*.—Abel ſpeaks :

Quel buon paftor fon io
Che tanto il gregge apprezza,
Che, per là fua falvezza,
Offre fe fteffo ancor.

I am that good fhepherd, who fo loves his flock, that, in defence of it, he offers his own life.

Conofco

Conofco ad una ad una
Le miè dilette agnelle;
E riconofcon quelle
Il tenero paftor.

I know one by one my pretty little lambs; and they, in return, know each their tender fhepherd.

LETTER

LETTER VII.

My Lord,

FROM what has been said of the foregoing claffes, it is evident, that none of them are at all calculated to exprefs any emotion which approaches to agitation. Their peculiar characteriftics, dignity, tendernefs, elegance, are fuitable to the more temperate and finer feelings; their fubject, in fhort, is fentiment rather than paffion.

fion. This laft, however, affords yet
a very wide field for mufical expreffion ; and, perhaps, it is not going too
far to fay, that the more violent the
paffion, the more apt the expreffion of
it is to receive additional energy from
the power of mufic. The kind of airs
which go under the general denomination of *aria parlante* is that whofe
peculiar province is to exprefs violent
emotions of all kinds. As, on the one
hand, the neceffary connection between
the fubject of the *portamento,* the *cantabile,* and the *aria di mezzo carattere,*
with the refpective length of notes,
and, of confequence, flownefs of meafure, which has been mentioned as
characteriftic of each of thefe claffes,

is

is evident; fo, on the other hand, the incompatibility of emotions, in any degree violent, with flow and deliberate utterance, is equally evident. The circumstance, from which this clafs takes its denomination, being the acceleration of fpeech, common to all emotions whatever of the impetuous kind, it comprehends, of confequence, a vaft variety with refpect both to quality and degree:—It may be faid to take up expreflion juft where the *aria di mezzo carattere* leaves it. Some airs of this laft clafs, of the livelieft caft, may approach indeed fo near to fome of the *parlante* of the leaft agitated kind, that it might, perhaps, be difficult to fay to which clafs they belonged; but, as foon

as

as the expreffion begins to be in any degree impetuous, the diftinction is evident, as the degree of paffion to be expreffed increafes the air, affumes the
name of *aria agitata, aria di ftrepito,
aria infuriata.* Expreffions of fear, of
joy, of grief, of rage, when at all impetuous, to their higheft and moft frantic degrees, are all comprehended under the various fubdivifions of the
clafs.—Their rhythm has its peculiar
province, the effect of this kind of airs
depending, perhaps, chiefly on its powers. The inftrumental parts are here
likewife of great efficacy, particularly
in the expreffion of the more violent
paffions, giving, by the addition of a
great body of found, and by the di-
ftinctnefs

ftinctnefs and rapidity of their execution, a force and energy to the whole,
which could never be the effect of a
voice alone, however flexible, however
powerful ; and if it be allowed, that the
beating of a drum has, in confequence of
certain principles of found and rhythm,
a confiderable effect on the mind, and
that ten drums have a proportionably
greater effect than one, it muft, I ap-
prehend, be alfo allowed, that founds
more beautiful, and as diftinct, nay,
infinitely more capable, from their duration, to mark the rhythm by diftin-
guifhing paufe from length of note,
muft have a fimilar effect on the mind,
—finer, however, and more powerful,
in proportion to their fuperior beauty,

L   accu-

accuracy, and other advantages. The inftruments here, far from ,being re-ftricted to the mere fupport of the voice, are called in to co-operate with it in producing one and the fame ef-fect, but with greater power than that which could be produced by the voice alone.

I am well aware, it may be objected here, that the greater the force of the inftruments the more they will be apt to overpower the voice, and, of confe-quence, to deftroy the principal fource of expreffion, namely, the fenfe of con-nection between the words and the notes; and, perhaps, it may not be very eafy to convince thofe, who are

not

not converfant with mufic, how it is
poffible this fhould not be the cafe.
All thofe, however, who have been accuftomed to hear good mufic well performed, will be fatisfied, on recollec-
tion, that, in this kind of airs, they
have often heard a very numerous orcheftra exert all its powers, without in
the leaft covering the voice, or difgui-
fing the fenfe : And the reafon is fimply this, that what is called the " for-
" tiffimo," or extreme fórce of the orcheftra, is not continued uniformly
throughout the accompanyment, which
would, indeed, have the effect of completely drowning the voice,—but that
this extreme exertion is inftantaneouf-
ly called forth, either in thofe particu-

lar

lar notes which are peculiarly fignifi-
cant of the rhythm, fuch as the firft of
the bar, &c. or on fome note or notes
where the fenfe itfelf requires it; after
which the *piano* or *hufh* of the orcheftra immediately takes place, bearing
the voice, excepting in fuch inftanta-
neous lightnings of found, if I may be
allowed the expreffion, eminently fuperior throughout, nor ever playing for
any length of time with the fame continued, or with increafing force, excepting in the cafe of fome climax in
the expreffion, where the words have
either been already heard, or in which,
at leaft, their fenfe, even were they not
diftinctly heard, cannot, from the general tenor of the air, be miftaken.

This

This extraordinary fwell from all the parts of the orcheftra is, in general, practifed with great fuccefs at the conclufion of fuch airs, in which, fuppofing the words even not to be underftood, (any further than they can be gueffed at from the context, and by the action of the fpeaker), the effect they are intended to have on the audience is more happily obtained than it could be by the clear articulation of them, unaccompanied by that torrent of paffion, if I may fo fpeak, which may be produced by this united exertion of all the inftrumental parts.—For it muft be likewife obferved that paffion, when very violent, is expreffed not fo much by the words of the fpeak-

er

er as by other figns,—the tones of the voice, the action of the face, and the gefture; infomuch, that I am confident I have heard many airs of this kind, in which, had the actor, without fpeaking a note, looked and acted his part with propriety, nobody would have been at a lofs to judge either of the kind or of the degree of paffion by which he feem-ed actuated. Rouffeau, fomewhere in his works, makes a very ingenious ob-fervation, the truth of which the Italian compofers feem evidently to have felt, —That, as violent paffion has a ten-dency to choak the voice, fo, in the expreffion of it by mufical founds, a *roulade*, which is a regular fucceffion of notes up or down, or both, rapidly

pro-

pronounced on one vowel, has often a
more powerful effect than diftinct articulation :—Such paffages are fometimes introduced in airs of this kind ;
and, though I cannot help giving my
affent to Rouffeau's obfervation, yet I
muft, at the fame time, confefs, that
they are too apt to be abufed, and that,
if continued for any length of time,
they have always appeared to me unnatural. Upon the whole, I hope,
however, it muft be evident, even to
thofe who are not converfant with mufic, that, in the expreffion of the more
violent paffions, the inftrumental parts
may have a greater latitude than in o-
ther kinds of airs, in which the emotions being more moderate, the expreffion

fion of them depends proportionally more on the force of the words, and lefs on the tone and action with which they are accompanied. But, whatever may be the effect of airs of this kind, when properly led by the circumftances of the piece and explained by the character of the fpeaker, your Lordfhip muft fee with what impropriety they are introduced, as is frequently the cafe, in our concerts, where, without the audience being apprifed either of the intereft of the piece, or the nature of the characters, they are fung by a fellow ftanding bolt upright, with one hand in his fide, and the other in his breeches-pocket, and where, into the bargain, the unmerciful fcrapers of our

orcheftra

orcheftra, taking the advantage of the *fortiffimo*, which they find now and then written above the notes of their parts, feem to vie with one another, who fhall moft effectually overpower, throughout, both the voice of the finger, and the melody of the fong. It is this kind of ignorant felection, and murderous execution, which give fenfible people a diftafte to Italian mufic in general; nor can they furely be blamed for thinking it abfurd, that a man fhould fay what cannot, in the nature of things, be heard, and that all that violent fracas and noife of inftruments is a moft ridiculous accompanyment to the affected immobility and unmeaning fimper of the finger.

M But

But to return to the subject;—your Lordship will perceive, that between those most violent expressions, and those that are least so, which this class comprehends, there must be an almost infinite variety, in respect both of kind and degree. I shall, therefore, content myself with giving your Lordship examples of the principal divisions only, and shall begin by that kind which I mentioned before as taking up expression, where the *aria di mezzo carattere* leaves it, and as being of this nature, that it might even be sometimes difficult to decide which of these classes it belonged to.

Del sen gli ardori
Nessun mi vanti :
Non soffro amori ;
Non voglio amanti ;
Troppo miè cara
La libertà.

Let no one boast to me the ardours of his
bosom : I suffer not loves ; I am adverse to
lovers ; my liberty is too dear to me.

Se fosse ognuno
Cosi sincero,
Meno importuno
Sarrebbe il vero
Saria pui rara
L' infedeltà.

If every one were as sincere, truth would
be less offensive, and infidelity more rare.

If

If the words of this air were put in the mouth of a gay young girl, thus carefully fignifying her infenfibility to ove and her defire of liberty, it might with propriety be fo compofed as to rank with the Airs *di mezzo carattere*, and would be well expreffed by that pleafing, though unimpaffioned, can-tileno, which is characteriftic of that clafs. But if, on the other hand, we fuppofe them fpoken with a degree of earneftnefs to an importunate lover, in order to get rid of him, it muft, in that cafe, certainly be fo compofed as to belong to the firft divifion of the *aria parlante.*

In

In the following example no such uncertainty can take place, the degree of paſſion, or of intereſt, at leaſt, ex-preſſed by it, referring it plainly to this laſt claſs : Achilles ſpeaks it, about to leave Deidamia :

Dille che ſi confoli,
Dille che m' ami e dille,
Che partì fido Achille
Che fido tornerà.

Tell her to be comforted ; tell her to love me ; and tell her, that Achilles left her faith-ful, that faithful he will return.

Che a ſuoi bei occhi ſoli
Fia che 'l mio cor ſi ſtempre
Che l' idol mio fù ſempre
Che l' idol mio farà.

That

That her charms alone fhall have the fo-
vereignty of my heart; that fhe ever was,
that fhe ever fhall, be my only love.

In order to be as explicit as poffible,
I fhall give your Lordfhip two other
examples from the fame piece, which,
with regard to the expreffion, feem
nearly equal in degree, though widely
different in kind.—Deidamia, reproach-
ing Achilles for want of affection, fays :

> No, ingrato, amor non fenti;
> O fe pur fenti amore,
> Perder non vuoi del cor,
> Per me la pace.

No, ungrateful! thou feeleft not love; or
if, indeed, thou feeleft it, thou art not willing,
for my fake, to lofe the peace of thy bofom.

Amai;

Amai; fe te 'l rammenti,
E puoi fenza penar,
Amare e difamar
Quando ti piace.

Perhaps thou loveft; but remember, thou can'ft not love, and, without pain, ceafe to love at pleafure.

The other is put in the mouth of Achilles, on his fufpicion of being deprived of his miftrefs by a rival:

Il volarmi il mio teforo!
Ah dov' è queft' alma ardita?
A da togliermi la vita
Che vuol togliermi il mio ben.

Rob me of my treafure! Ah, where is this
pre-

prefumptuous foul? He muſt firſt take my life
who would rob me of my love.

M' avvilifce in queſte ſpoglie
Il poter di due pupille;
Ma lo ſo ch'io ſono Achille,
Ma mi ſento Achille in fen.

The power of too bright eyes difgraces me
in theſe weeds; but I know—I feel, that I am
Achilles.

Though the general acceleration of
ſpeech common to each of theſe Airs,
and which, therefore, brings them under the ſame claſs, be, perhaps, nearly
equal in both, yet the ſkilful compoſer
will nicely difcriminate, not only between the warlike audacity of Achilles,
and

and the feminine foftnefs of Dudanio, but alfo between the expreffion of dif-appointed affection in the former, and of jealous refentment in the latter.

I beg leave to offer the two follow-ing examples alfo, as approaching, in degree, to the foregoing, though very different in kind; the firft par-taking fomewhat of the tendernefs which is characteriftic of the *cantabile ;* the fecond of the dignity which belongs to the *portamento.*

Parto, non ti fdegnar;
Si madre mia da te;
Gli affetti a moderar
Queft' alma impara.

N

I go, be not offended; yes, my mother, I go; this foul fhall learn from thee to moderate its affections.

Gran Colpa pur non è
Se mal frenar fi pŭò,
Un figlio che perdè
Un figlio che trovò
Si cara madre.

Surely it is no heinous fault that a fon can-not eafily command himfelf, who loft, who found, fo dear a mother.

In the following Air, Xerxes, on being reconciled to Themiftocles, thus addreffes him:

Contrafto affai piú degno,
Se vuoi, comincierà;

Or

Or che la gloria in noi
L'odio in amor cambio.

A much nobler combat, if thou wilt, fhall commence betwixt us; now that glory has changed our hatred into love.

Scordati tu lo fdegno
Jo le vendette obblio
Tú mio foftegno ed io
Tuo difenfor faro.

Forget there thy enmity, I will bury in oblivion my refentment; thou fhalt be my fupport, I will be thy protector.

In the following examples, the violence of the expreffion being increafed, the mufic affumes the denomination of *aria agitata.*

L'alma

L'alma delira,
Par che manchino
Quasi i respiri,
Che fuor del petto
Mi balza il cor.

My soul grows delirious with excessive joy;
I pant for breath, my heart seems to jump
from my bosom.

Quant' è piu facile
Ch'un gran diletto
Giunga ad uccidere
Che un gran dolor.

How much more apt is excess of joy to kill,
than excess of grief.

I cannot pass by this example, however, without observing to your Lordship,

ſhip, that the ſecond part of the Air, is by no means proper for muſical ex‧preſſion: It ceaſes to be the language of paſſion; and is, beſides, a reflection which no perſon, in ſuch a ſtate as the firſt part indicates, would naturally make. In ſetting the Opera to Muſic, a judicious compoſer would ſtrike it out altogether. The next example, though evidently different, with re‧gard to the kind of expreſſion, belongs to the ſame ſub‧diviſion of this claſs.

Gia l'idea del giuſto ſcempio
Mi rapiſce, mi diletta,
Gia penſando alla vendetta
Mi commincio a vendicar.

Already

Already the idea of the juſt ſlaughter de-
lights me; already, thinking of my vengeance,
I begin to be revenged.

Gia quel barbaro quel empio
Fa di ſangue il ſuol vermiglio
Ed il ſangue del mio figlio
Gia ſi ſente rin facciar.

I ſee the impious wretch already dye the
earth with his blood; already the murder of
my ſon ſtares him in the face.

The examples I am next to give
your Lordſhip, are of that kind which
takes the name of *aria di ſmanie*; for
which I do not recollect any phraſe in
Engliſh exactly equivalent: It is an
appellation given to the expreſſion of
ſuch emotions as take away, in ſome
degree,

degree, the right ufe of reafon, and
begin to border on infanity.

> Non vedi tiranno
> Ch' io moro d'affanno
> Che bramo che in pace
> Mi lafci morir.

Seeft thou not, tyrant, that I die of grief,
and only wifh thou wouldft fuffer me to die in
peace.

> Ch'o l'alma fi oppreffa
> Che tutto mi fpiace,
> Che quafi me fteffa
> Non poffo foffrir.

That my foul is fo oppreffed, that every
thing is hateful to me, that I can no longer
fuffer even myfelf.

Dimmi

Dimmi crudel dov' è:
Ah non tacer cofi.
Barbaro Ciel perchè
Infino a quefto di
Serbarmi in vita.

Tell me cruel—Where is fhe? Ah do not
thus be filent, barbarous Heaven! Ah, Why
didft thou prolong my life to this day.

Corrafi—Ah! dove? oh Dei!
Chi guida e paffi miei
Chi, almen, chi, per mercè
La via m' addita.

Let me run,—Where? oh God! Who will
guide my fteps; who, for pity's fake, will direct me?

Recitative.

RECITATIVE.

———Fuggi Sebaſte, ah dove
Fuggiro da me ſteſſo ? ah porto in ſeno
Il carnefice mio : dovunque vada
Il terror, lo ſpavento
Seguiran la mia traccia
La colpa mia, mi ſtarà ſempre in faccia.

Fly Sebaſte—ah whither ſhall I fly from
myſelf ? Alas ! I carry in my boſom my exe-
cutioner ; wherever I go horror follows my
ſteps ; my guilt muſt ever ſtare me in the face.

A I R.

Aſpri remorſi atroci
Figli del fallo mio
Perche ſi tardi, oh Dio !
Mi lacerate il cor.

O   Cruel

Cruel heart-rending remorfe, offspring of my crime; Why, oh God, fo late doft thou tear my bofom?

Perche funefte voci,
Ch'or mi fgridate appreffo,
Perche vi afcolto adeffo,
Ne v'afcoltar fin or?

Ye fatal voices, which now howl around me, if deaf to you hitherto, why do I liften to you now?

The laft divifion of this clafs of airs is that which is adapted to the expref-fion of paffion, of whatever kind, when become frantic; and is properly termed *aria infuriata*.

RECI-

RECITATIVE.

——Non più, Mandane,
Il mio furor mi avanza,
Non ifpirarmi il tuo, fremo abbaſtanza.

——No more, Mandane, infpire me not
with thine, my own fury is fufficient.

A I R.

Men bramofa di ſtragi funeſte,
Va fcorrendo l'Armene foreſte
Fera tigre che i figli perdè.

With lefs thirſt for blood and ſlaughter, the
fierce tyger, robbed of its young, fcours the
Armenian foreſts.

Ardo d'ira, di rabbia deliro
Smanio, fremo, non odo, non miro
Che le furie che porto con me.

My

My wrath confumes me, I rave, I rage, I hear and fee nothing but the furies, which I carry with myfelf.

Rendimi il figlio mio:
Ah! Mi fi fpezza il cor.;
Non fon piu madre, oh Dio;
Non ò piu figlio.

Give me back my fon;—oh, my heart burfts;—no longer am I a mother;—oh God, my child is no more.

Fra mille furori
Che calma non anno,
Fra mille timori
Che intorno mi ftanno,
Accender mi fento,
Mi fento gelar.

Surrounded

Surrounded by a thoufand furies which know no calm, by a thoufand terrors which inceffantly purfue me, by turns I freeze, I burn.

I hope I have been able, by the foregoing examples, to give your Lord-fhip fome idea of the nature, extent, and variety of this clafs of airs, as well as of the reafon why fo great a variety is comprehended under the fame ge-neral denomination; a circumftance which, without due attention to its caufe, would appear abfurd and con-tradictory. Before I conclude, it is proper to take notice to your Lordfhip, that the words of an air may be fo written, as to afford fubject for two, or even three, of the claffes hitherto mentioned,

mentioned, not in a mixed manner, but feverally, of which my memory furnifhes me with the following exam‐ ple:

Pria ch'io rieda al campo,
Penfa ch'io fon Romano;
Che d'una fpada il lampo,
No, non mi fa terror.

Before I return to the camp, remember I am a Roman; that I rejoice in danger of bat‐ tle.

Spofa, Signor, che affanno!
Deh tergi i vaghi rai
Che fol nel dirti addio
Vacilla il mio valor.

Spoufe,—Sir,—what mifery !—for pity's fake

fake dry up thefe tears; only, in bidding thee adieu, my conftancy is fhaken.

Empio deftin tiranno:
O cento fmanie in feno,
O cento furie al cor.

Cruel, barbarous fate; a thoufand torments rend my bofom; I have a thoufand furies in my heart.

This air, your Lordfhip fees, is divided into three different parts; the firft of which, exprefling dignity of fentiment, belongs to the *portamento*; the fecond, exprefling tendernefs, to the *cantabile*; and the third, exprefling rage, to the laft divifion of the *aria parlante*.

LETTER

LETTER VIII.

My Lord,

FROM what I have said of the *aria di portamento*, the *cantabile*, the *mezzo carattere*, and the different sub-divisions of the *aria parlante*, I hope I have, in some degree, made it plain to your Lordship, that there is no affection of the human breast, from the slightest and most gentle stirring of sentiment, to the most frantic degrees of

P   passion,

paſſion, which ſome one of theſe claſſes
is not aptly ſuited to expreſs. If this
be true, other claſſes muſt be either
bad or ſuperfluous: This, in fact, is
the caſe of the *aria di agilità*, or *aria
di bravura*, as it is ſometimes called;
in treating of which, it will be almoſt
ſufficient to repeat to your Lordſhip
the deſcription I gave of it in the
general enumeration of the different
claſſes: It is an air compoſed *chiefly*,
indeed too often *merely*, to indulge the
ſinger in the diſplay of certain powers
in the execution, particularly extraordinary agility or compaſs of voice.
In ſuch a compoſition, the *means* are
evidently confounded with the *end* of
the art; dexterity, (if I may be allowed

ed the expreffion), and artifice, inftead
of ferving as the inftruments, being
made the objeft of the work : Such
are the airs which, with us, we fo frequently obferve fung to ears erect, and
gaping mouths, whilft the heart, in ho-
neft apathy, is carrying on its mere
animal function : And of this kind, indeed, are all the attempts, in the different arts, to fubftitute what is difficult or novel for what is beautiful
and natural. Where there has ever
been a genuine tafte for any of the arts,
this aptnefs to admire what is new and
difficult is one of the firft fymptoms of
the decline of that tafte; fuch is at
prefent the cafe in Italy with refpect to
all the arts; but the admiration be-
stowed

stowed in Britain on difficulty and novelty, in preference to beauty and fimplicity, is the effect, not of the decline,
but of the total want of taste, and proceeds from the same principles with the
admiration of tumbling and rope-
dancing, which the multitude may gaze
on with astonishment long before they
are susceptible of the charms of graceful and elegant pantomime, these feats
of agility having exactly the same relation to fine dancing that the above
mentioned airs have to expressive mufic: They are, therefore, I conceive,
incompatible with the nature of a ferious drama ; but in the burletta, or
comic opera, in which much greater
liberties may be taken, I think I have,
fome-

fometimes, heard them introduced with fuccefs. In a comedy, a pretty frolic-fome coquette may be fuppofed to cut an elegant caper, at once to fhow her legs and to difplay her fkill in dancing; nay, fuch a ftroke might be characte-riftic, and therefore proper: So a gay fafhionable lady might, with a kind of graceful levity, exprefs, by an air of this kind, fome of her pretty capricious humours, equally unintelligible with the mufic itfelf, the merit of both con-fifting merely in the prettinefs of the *manner*; for this kind of mufic, tho' incapable of any expreffion excepting that, perhaps, of gaiety in general, may yet have all the beauty which can be given to it by a fine voice running,

with

with eafe and velocity, though an ar-
rangment of notes, not in itfelf un-
pleafing, juft as the humour of the
lady, though perhaps rather unmeaning, may be accompanied with many
graces of countenance, figure, voice,
and motion.

Now, the union of all this with the
mufic, produces often, without any violation of propriety, a very happy effect on the ftage; but your Lordfhip
will obferve with what abfurd impropriety thefe airs often make a part of
our concerts, where all this elegant
flirtation of face and figure is forbid-
den, and where thefe fanciful and ex-
uberant fallies are gravely pronounced

by

by a lady ſtanding at the harpſicord
with downcaſt, or, at beſt, unmeaning
eyes, and without the ſmalleſt apparent
tendency to motion.

LETTER

LETTER IX.

___

My Lord,

I HAVE now endeavoured to give your Lordſhip as diſtinct an idea as I could of the ſimple and accompanied Recitative, and of all thoſe claſſes of Airs which have names in Italian, and which I mentioned in the firſt general enumeration I made of them. There is, however, another ſpecies of Airs, which I have not claſſed with

Q   them,

them, becaufe it has no particular denomination, though it appears to me
well deferving of that diftinction: But
this is eafily accounted for, when it is
confidered, as I took occafion to obferve in the beginning, that the names
of thefe claffes are all taken from circumftances of the practical part of the
art. The Airs alluded to here are thofe
whofe fubject is a fimile, and which I
fhall venture to call Airs of Imitation:
Thefe, though effentially different from
all thofe before mentioned, yet, from
fome circumftance of fimilarity in the
practical part, have been referred to
one or other of the above claffes.

Though,

Though, upon the whole, fimiles of any length be perhaps feldom admiffible in dramatic poetry, being in general repugnant to the genuine expreffion of paffion, yet fometimes they may be introduced without impropriety, more particularly in the mufical drama, which, like all the other arts, juftly claims fome licenfe in practice, with refpect to that beauty which is its chief object, or that fpecies of pleafure which it is peculiarly calculated to infpire.

Now, the greateft poffible variety of mufical effect being exactly the perfection of this kind of drama, and thofe Airs which have for their fubject a fimile, by giving fcope to the defcriptive

powers

powers of Mufic, being a fource of great beauty and variety to the piece, a more frequent introduction of fimiles may, on this principle, be allowed in the opera than in dramatic works, unaccompanied by mufic. Before I proceed to give your Lordfhip any examples of this Air, I beg leave to fay fomething on the principle of Mufical Imitation in general. And, firft, it is evident, that, befides the relations of acute and grave, of loud and foft, of continuous and difcontinuous, which are fimply the fame in noife of all kinds, as in mufical founds, there are many circumftances of refemblance between thefe laft and other founds, for fome of which we have not even names. The

found

found of a little flute, for example, re-
fembles the finging of birds, not from
its fhrillnefs merely, but on account of
a certain quality of found common to
both, which every ear is fenfible of,
but which we have no words to exprefs.
It is by this quality of found that we diftinguifh the voices of perfons, though
fpeaking, perhaps nearly on the fame
pitch, and difcriminate different inftruments while playing the fame mufical
notes; and the Italians have, therefore,
very properly termed it *il metallo della
voce.* Again, motion in bodies, though
not common to motion in mufic, in all
its extent, is, in fome refpects, the
fame; in others fimilar, or at leaft a-
nalogous: Slow and quick, with regard

gard to fucceffion, with all the poffible
degrees between their perceptible extremes, are common to both : The
fame may be faid of regular and irregular ; and, where thefe fail, analogies
can be affected by different means, as
ftriking as circumftances of pofitive
famenefs or refemblance. Gliding, as
it is fometimes practifed, both by the
voice and by certain inftruments, is
the fame in mufic as in bodies, it being
in reality the effect of that motion in
fome body acting on another. The
notes of mufic, however, being each,
by its nature, ftationary, cannot, ftrictly
fpeaking, be faid to glide ; yet the idea
of a gliding motion is eafily conveyed
by a certain arrangement of notes :
In

In the fame manner, foaring, finking, and even level motion, are equally eafily expreffed; and though, to be fure, a note cannot be faid to turn or run round like a body, yet a fucceffion of notes may be found that may give an idea of circular motion, the difference between thefe motions in mufic and in bodies being fomething like the difference between thefe circles

Setting afide then the more obfcure analogies in mufic, which are felt, perhaps, only in confequence of a certain

orga-

organization, or a degree of imagination not common to all men, it is furely evident, that refemblances or analogies may be produced, by means of
founds, and of their rythm and arrangement, to every thing in nature,
which we perceive in confequence of
found and motion : Thus the whiftling
of the winds, the noife of thunder, the
roaring and dafhing of the fea, the
murmurs of a ftream, the whifpers of
the breeze,—the folemn waving of a
lofty pine, the forked motion and mo-
mentary appearance of lightning, the
grand fwell of a billow, the rapidity of
a torrent, the meanders of a rivulet,
or the fmooth gliding of a filent ftream,
muft, even to thofe who have not a
musical

muſical ear, appear all within the compaſs of muſical imitation; for this
plain reaſon, that poſitive reſemblance
is, in faƈt, the ground of this imitation. Nor does the analogy ſeem much
ſtrained, when we ſay that muſic may
imitate the tread of a giant, the light
and nimble footſteps of a nymph, or
even the motion of thoſe fanciful beings
whom Shakeſpeare has deſcribed as
" chaſing, with printleſs feet, the eb-
" bing Neptune." But the imitation
of which muſic is capable is not ſtinted
to ſuch poſitive reſemblances as thoſe
now cited; general ideas of hugeneſs
and immenſity, of lightneſs and elegance, of operations that are performed
with difficulty or with facility, of or-

der, of confufion, of exertion, of repofe, of energy, of debility, of fimilarity, of difcrepancy, of union, of incompatibility, and many more, may be
clearly conveyed by different qualities,
modifications, arrangements, rythm,
and combinations of mufical founds.
With refpect to the more diftant and
obfcure analogies, fuch as that to cold,
light, darknefs, pain, and the like, as,
to thofe who are lefs fenfible of 'the
effects of mufic, they may feem to ori-
ginate rather in the enthufiafm of the
hearer than in any reality in the art,
I fhall not infift on them.

I hope, upon the whole, your Lordfhip will agree with me that it is evident

dent that there are fufficient grounds to go upon to juftify the attempt of i-mitative mufic as diftinct from paffion-ate; and that the introduction of airs of this laft kind muft, in confequence of the variety they give, tend to beau-tify the whole, and render it more complete. I muft confefs, however, that I have often feen them ufed too frequently in the fame piece; and that the effect of them can never be com-pletely fine when they are not dictated by, and accompanied throughout, with fome fentiment or paffion of the fpeak-er.—The following is an example in point.

RECI-

RECITATIVE.

——In ogni forte
L'iſteſſa è la virtù ; l'agita è vero,
Il nemico deſtin, ma non l'opprime ;
E quando e men felice, è piu ſublime.

In every ſtate virtue is the ſame; adverſe
fate, it is true, agitates, but cannot oppreſs it;
and when it is leaſt happy, it is then moſt ſublime.

AIR.

Quercia annoſa, ſu l'erte pendici,
Fra il contraſto di venti nemici,
Piu ſecura, piu ſalda ſi fa.

The knotted oak, which, high on the rug-
ged cliffs, braves the contending winds, be-
comes by them more firm and more ſecure.

Che

Che s'el verno di chiome le sfronda,
Piu nel fuolo col piè fi profonda,
Forza aquifta, fe perde belta.

And if the winter defpoils it of its leaves, it makes it fink deeper in the earth its roots, and it acquires ftrength in proportion as it lofes beauty.

In the foregoing example, the image of the oak itfelf on the high cliffs, the raging of the winds, and the dignity of the fentiment in the fpeaker, all confpire to produce the fame effect of grandeur. But I have feen airs, in which the fubject of the paffionate part was different from that of the imitative, fo contrived, as to keep each moft di-ftinctly feparate from the other, whilft,

at

at the fame time, the union of both
made one beautiful whole. Handel,
in his Oratorio of Acis and Galatea,
has produced a mafter-ftroke of this
kind.—Galatea, addreffing herfelf to
the birds that are fuppofed to be finging around her, fays,

Hufh, hufh, ye little warbling quire,
Your thrilling ftrains
Awake my pains,
And kindle fierce defire.

In this example, there is no comparifon made; the imitative part is only
fuggefted by the fenfe, and the compofer has taken the hint in adapting
the mufic to it, and has indeed done
it

it with the utmoft propriety as well as
ingenuity. It is plain, in this air,
that, if the imitation of any thing is
to be at all attempted, it muft be that
of the warbling quire: And it is as
plain, that the paffionate expreffion of
the fpeaker has not even the moft diftant relation to the finging of birds;
—to have fet the voice a finging, in
imitation of the birds, or, whilft the
voice fang the paffionate part, to have
made the birds fing either in unifon,
or in direct harmony, with the voice,
would have been each equally abfurd.
It would feem, indeed, at firft fight,
almoft impoffible to reconcile two
things fo different; yet this great genius, by confining each part to its pro-

per .

per province, has fo artfully managed
the compofition, that, whilft the vocal
part moft feelingly fpeaks ·the paffion,
a little flagellet from the orcheftra carries on, throughout, the delightful
warbling of the quire, and though perfectly different in found, melody, and
rythm, from the notes fung by the
voice, inftead of diftracting the attention from it, or confounding the expreffion, ferves to add new beauty and
grace to the effect; juft as your Lordfhip may conceive a naked figure fo
veiled with fome light and tranfparent
veftment floating to the wind, as at
once completely to reveal the figure,
and, by its undulating folds, add new
charms both to the motion and the
form.

form. Nothing can put in a stronger
light the discrimination which I before
made to your Lordship, of the passion-
ate and imitative powers of music,
than the above mentioned air, or more
clearly evince the propriety of assign-
ing the first to the voice alone, and of
confining the instruments to the other
only. This principle, indeed, long before it was perhaps ever thought of,
either by philosophers or composers,
must have been generally felt; and
even the powers of the great Handel
could not compensate its violation in
composition; for, in the very same
opera, a little after, when Galatea is
made to convert Acis into a stream,
and, after the symphony has made a

S   fine

fine imitation of the winding of the ftream through the vale, he makes Galatea repeat it with her voice; and, though the mufic of the air be, in other refpects, beautiful in the extreme, yet I do not believe it was ever performed without appearing tedious, even to thofe who never dreamed of this principle; and, to thofe who were acquainted with it, at once tedious and abfurd.

In the firft example I gave your Lordfhip of thefe airs of imitation, the comparifon is itfelf the fubject, and the nature of the fentiment coinciding perfectly with it, only ferves to increafe, perhaps, the general pathos, without forming.

forming, in any degree, a feparate fubject.—The fecond contains plainly a double fubject, contrived with wonderful art to go on together, to fet off each other, and to form one beautiful whole. There is ftill a third kind of thefe airs, that holds a middle place between thofe two, in which, there being no exprefs comparifon, the imitative part, as in the laft, is only fuggefted by the words, but being, as in the firft, of the fame quality, as it were, with the fentiment, does not make the immediate fubject of the mufic, but is kept fubordinate to the expreffion of the paffion or fentiment. The following air is of this fpecies :

Intendo

'Intendo, amico rio;
Quel baſſo mormorio
Tu chiedi in tua favella
Il noſtro ben dov' è.

I underſtand thee, gentle river ; in that
plaintive murmur, thou inquireſt with me
where our love is gone.

As the compariſons which make the
ſubjeƐt of theſe airs, or, as the objeƐts
of which they only ſuggeſt the imitation, may be ſublime, elegant, gay,
boiſterous, &c. ſo they may ſeverally
have a relation to ſome one or other
of the claſſes before mentioned, the
portamento, the cantabile, the mezzo carattere, and the different diviſions of
the aria parlante, —and, of conſequence,

·quence, may be referred to them; the divifion which I have made of mufic into paffionate and imitative being rather of a philofophical kind, whilft that by which the Italians have formed the different claffes of their airs originates, as I have faid, in circumftances of practice only. So juft is their divifion, that, to give a diftinct idea of any of thefe airs, we muft fay it is an air of imitation of the *portamento* ftile, or of the *cantabile*, &c.

F I N I S.